Shyness

How To Overcome Shyness and Social Anxiety Own Your Mind, Confidence and Happiness

2nd Edition

By
Sofia Price

Sofia Price

Table of Contents

Sofia Price

Introduction

I want to thank you and congratulate you for purchasing this book, *"Shyness: How To Overcome Shyness and Social Anxiety: Own Your Mind, Confidence and Happiness."*

This book contains proven steps and strategies on how to cure yourself of your shyness.

Shyness may hinder people from participating in many things, even those that they like. Thus, shyness could effectively get in the way of happiness. Whether you are searching for ways to just gain a little confidence or to completely overcome shyness, this book will help you.

Thanks again for purchasing this book, and I hope you enjoy it!

Chapter 1 – Shyness 101

Shyness. You hear it so often but if I ask you what does it really mean, can you be specific? Well, one way to define it is that is that it is a personality characteristic that makes it very hard for a person to establish a good rapport with the people he or she gets to meet. Other people experience shyness as simply being tongue-tied in social gatherings, i.e., doesn't know what to say. For some, it may be a bit more severe, with physical manifestations such as sweating or shallow breathing and weakened voice. But for most people, it's a combination of many other seemingly harmless symptoms that vary in degrees.

People who aren't really shy find it quite easy to do certain things like making eye contact, standing in a straight and relaxed manner, engage in small talk and smile. On the other hand, shy people find such things to be quite a challenge. In fact, the mere thought of having to do them can make shy people really uneasy because it's not natural for them.

Being shy isn't just about being tongue-tied. As mentioned, even simple things like smiling at others or making eye contact can be hard for them. As such, when shy people do their best to do them, they can be perceived as people who are not sincere.

So how does shyness really look like? Here are some behaviors that are symptomatic of shyness:

-Being anxious and unconfident in the presence of others;

-Having a hard time carrying a conversation or making small talk;

-Behaving awkwardly in social gatherings due to ignorance of expected social behaviors;

-Inability to maintain eye contact, stand confidently straight or even smile;

-Having to force one's self to attend social gatherings such as reunions, parties, wakes, group discussions and meetings, among others.

There are moments that shyness can be confused for phobias, which are behavior-crippling and irrational habits or actions. For example, we know that generally speaking, fear of people is rather foolish. We're also aware that people will most likely like us if they see we are cheerful, relaxed and confident instead of being gloomy, rigid and unconfident. For some reason, though, we seem to have the innate tendency to act in particular ways. Though the kind of fear involved in legit phobias is rather extreme, shyness and phobia do have some things in common, although in differing degrees.

Is It A Sin To Be Shy?

It seems that there are perceptions that being shy is equivalent to being sick – that shyness is a disease. Truth is, it isn't a sickness and shy people aren't "sick". Those who think otherwise may be the ones who actually have a problem with shyness. For one, some of the most kind-hearted people happen to be, well, shy! And if you take a look at the world's most evil and despicable people, you'll be hard-pressed to find shy ones. Hitler wasn't shy. Mussolini wasn't shy. Osama Bin Laden certainly wasn't shy.

Shy people also happen to be some of the most humble people I've met. Well, it's practically impossible to be puffed up with pride if you don't think of yourself highly, right? Shy people also seem to be highly unlikely to be demanding, abrasive, aggressive, overbearing or hostile. Shy people can make for really loyal friends because they work harder to keep friendships, as these come by very seldom for them. They're also more unassuming and discreet.

If there's one thing that shy people generally tend to be really good at compared to confident ones, it's with the art of listening because let's face it, they don't dominate conversations because they usually find it hard to talk. As such, many shy people tend to understand others better. They're some of the best team members to have around because they normally don't struggle to control groups and situations.

With all the generally good qualities of shy people, why then isn't shyness considered a real virtue? Or why aren't shy people as popular or as well liked as those who are confident? Well, it's because people are hard-wired to be drawn towards people who are confident – people who can lead, people who can eloquently express themselves and ideas and people who can take control.

Most shy people may look at their shyness as a good attribute, which can be a reasonable proposition. However, shyness may not be in and of itself good or bad but depending on its severity, it has the ability to keep people from living life to the fullest on one end and from living normally at all on the other extreme.

For example, it may not be bad to be courteous and respectful, as most shy people are but it can get in the way of your being able to enjoy your life. Imagine for a moment you are meet a very beautiful woman through a very good friend. She's very friendly, lively, fun and engaging. Plus, she seems to be a person who's very down to earth!

Shyness may keep you from getting to know her better if for example you too are tongue-tied to even ask things about her, like what she does for a living or where she's from, among other things. Yes, being shy doesn't make you an evil person but there are some beautiful life moments that you may miss out on because of it.

Again, there's nothing inherently wrong with being shy – only the degree to which it keeps you from truly embracing life and enjoying it to the fullest.

How Un-Shy People View Shy Ones

Pardon me for the use of the word "un-shy" as there really isn't a word like that. I just used it for illustration purposes. Let's just use this to refer to outgoing people, shall we?

As I mentioned earlier, confident or outgoing people naturally attract people to them. That's the way it is. But those who aren't really aware of what being shy is all about may not understand why shy people aren't drawn to them. In fact, they may not see that in general, shy people aren't drawn to anyone in particular, except probably for their family and closest friends. As such, many un-shy people tend to be aloof around shy people – even having ill feelings towards them.

Because of such an impression, many shy people may feel that they are "abnormal" or that something's just not right with them. Worse, they may feel less important than un-shy people – that they're second-class citizens of the world. It can be quite difficult to be disliked just because you're shy despite your being a really good person. Probably it's because of most people's tendencies to see the negatives more than the positives.

Another thing going against shy people is the perception that the reason for their lack of self-confidence is the lack of anything to be confident about. It's as if shy people are automatically deemed as uninteresting, boring or worse, incompetent. It's as if shyness is a placard posted on one's forehead saying "I'm not worth being with." Nothing can be so far from the truth as that.

The real problem lies with the false perceptions and not shyness itself. In the same manner that confidence can sometimes be judged as arrogance, especially in cultures where being shy and bashful is the cultural norm, culture and perception is what's wrong with the ill reputations attached to being shy. If there's any real negative effect of shy people on other shyness that's quite legit is that shy people's shyness can make un-shy people shy around them. Yes – shyness at some point can be contagious!

There's some science that can actually vouch for it. A research that was published in The Journal Of Personality And Social Psychology conducted by Avril Thorne found that when both their extrovert and introvert subjects were paired together, the initially significant personality differences were reduced. It seems that lack of feedback from the shy partner led to the un-shy one's loss for words.

The research highlights why un-shy people usually have a not-so-stellar perception of shy ones – they start to feel shy themselves. And with the general impression about shy people, e.g., they're either boring, uninteresting or worse, incompetent, it's not surprising why un-shy people shudder at the thought of feeling shy themselves.

To Reveal Or Not To Reveal You Secret Shy-Dentity

Many well-meaning people will encourage you to be honest and upfront with practically anyone you meet or get into contact with – announce your shyness. Why? The noble reason for suggesting such is to help the un-shy people understand why you may behave or talk the way you do, which can hopefully bridge the gap between you and the un-shy person. But regardless of the noble intentions behind it, is such an advice a wise one?

The answer is, it really depends on the person. If for example, most people have the impression that you're aloof and cold because of your shyness, you can help change such a negative perception by matter-of-factly saying "Being around cool people like y'all make me really shy, y'know?" Just beware that this kind of approach may not work for every un-shy person you come into contact with, particularly those who simply view shy people as boring and un-interesting. With such a perception, it's highly unlike for such people to feel empathy towards you, which isn't your problem anymore but theirs.

There are instances too, where being upfront about your shyness can be the worst thing you can ever say. This is because eliciting empathy from the un-shy people has a 50% chance of happening while the other 50% can lead to the making them feel that you can be a really difficult person to talk to and thus, become a self-sabotaging strategy.

Although telling the un-shy people upfront is neither right nor wrong, it's much better to develop the skill of making small talk despite your uneasiness to do so. It's because being able to do so is the only sure fire way to dispel any notion of you being someone who's difficult to talk to and unfriendly.

Naturally Shy Or Conditioned To Be One?

Some evidences suggest that shyness can be due to nature or genetic and is inherited from our folks. One research – done by Jerome Kagan, a Harvard University psychologist – discovered that some adults' shyness have already manifested as early as 3 years old. One argument raised by skeptics is that by the time a child turns 3, he or she may have already received enough social and parental conditioning that lead to their exhibiting shyness at such an age. Kagan and his colleagues then conducted a similar research – this time on 2-year-old children – to see if shyness is learned instead of being inborn or genetic. The results were the same – 20% of the 2-year old subjects exhibited shyness.

Because critics still abound, Kagan and his colleagues did another study of the same kind but this time, the subjects included 4-year old infants! Once again, the some of the subjects exhibited shyness, leading Kagan to conclude that part of the genetic reason for it is the nervous system. In laymen's terms, a person's brain physiology can make certain people pre-disposed to being shy. And going back to Kagan's study, tracking the children subjects' growth revealed that those who exhibited shyness earlier on continued to exhibit the same even at 7 years old. Other researches also established a biological link to the trait. For example, in one study, identical twin subjects were more likely to exhibit the same trait than fraternal ones.

Now, this doesn't mean that all shyness is biological. No, no , no! It simply means that shyness CAN BE biological, which implies that it can also be due to environmental conditioning. In fact, Kagan's researches showed that only about 1/3 of really shy children seemed were so because of genetics.

Now, is it possible to un-shy yourself if you're naturally pre-disposed to being shy? The answer is a resounding...YES!!! It's worth noting people who aren't genetically predisposed to being extroverts can become so. This is because personalities can be developed and modified, just as with skills like playing musical instruments and painting. Just keep this in mind – genetics isn't equal to fate. If you're shy, biologically or through conditioning, be hopeful that you don't need to be shy for the rest of your life and that you can do something about it.

If you're shy (I suppose you are because after all, you bought this book), I'd like to encourage you to be easy on yourself. Don't take the blame for being so and certainly don't wallow in it. Doing so won't change a thing and may even make things worse. Don't try to shift the blame on others either, i.e., your parents or your environment. Simply put, don't blame. Just take responsibility for doing something about it. No use dwelling on the past and on the problem. It's best to focus on what can be done to change or manage it well.

Shy = Low Self-Esteem?

There's a prevalent myth about shyness that's been going around since time immemorial. In particular, that all shy people have low self-esteem or inferiority complex. Well, that's what it is – a myth.

Shyness is about how you respond to social situations. Being shy can – over time – lead to feeling inferior when it comes to relating with other people in general. However, this kind of inferiority isn't the cause of shyness but rather the fruit of it.

It's also incorrect to say that no shy people suffer from low self-esteem or inferiority complex because truth is, some of them have such conditions. The main point to remember is shyness and feelings of low self-esteem and inferiority complex aren't always on the same boat.

Shy = Selfish?

There's a school of thought that equates shyness to selfishness. Why is that so? These people argue that being shy is all about being too self-centered, i.e., what will people think of me, I don't' want to be ridiculed, etc. What these people are saying is that at the root of it, shyness is being self-absorbed...selfishness.

Although there's a bit of logic to that train of thought, I don't agree with it. First, it's so unfair to generalize shy people as selfish. They're already having a very hard time dealing with it and they don't need to worry about being branded as selfish on top of being perceived as boring and incompetent.

Second, it may be that some shy people are selfish, but it's obviously clear that not all of them are. If that weren't the case, then why not make the same case for confident people too? I mean, since some confident people are self-centered, doesn't it stand to reason that all of them are? My point exactly.

Besides, there's increasing evidence – as presented earlier – about how shyness in some people is actually biological. Further, it's becoming clear that in many cases, shyness is simply a result of lacking the skills for small talk or regular conversations as well as due to social conditioning, particularly shameful experiences growing up.

Not all shy people are selfish and not all selfish people are shy. 'Nuff said!

Shy = Introvert?

Some dictionaries define being an introvert as being more interested in one's own thoughts than in his surroundings. Another one explains introversion as focus of interest on self rather than others and that extroverts are people who are the opposite: more focused on others than himself. Honestly, those definitions are unfair because they put introverts in a bad light as people who are only concerned about themselves, i.e., selfish people. And that isn't a compliment at all, to say the least. If you look at some of the people who actually contributed much to the world, you'll find that many of them are introverts like Albert Einstein, Martin Luther, Sir Isaac Newton and Charles Darwin. Their efforts made our world a much better place. Now would you consider that self-centered?

The word introvert or introversion is also usually substituted for shy or shyness. However, these are 2 different personality types. For one, introverts love being alone, have very little desire to develop new friendships and can be perfectly happy and content without anyone else beside them. Shy people on the other hand, love to be with people and make new friends but aren't able to because of their shyness.

Another key difference is that shyness isn't something shy people choose to be. Introversion on the other hand, is a lifestyle choice.

Shy people are generally alone or have very few friends because they feel they don't have control over their shyness, which makes others uncomfortable with them and becomes a self-perpetuating cycle. Given a choice, shy people want to be with others and have many friends. Introverts choose not to be with most people and prefer to have very few friends.

It is possible for a shy person to have some introvert characteristics and vice versa but in the strictest sense, both are different. In fact, there are even shy extroverts – people who can carry conversations well with others and can turn on their charismatic personality despite feeling shy inside. Such people include Elizabeth Taylor, Rosalyn Carter, John Travolta and Johnny Carson.

Remember, shy is about how you feel inside and you can be an extrovert and draw people to you even if feel that way. How you relate to people externally matters more than what you feel inside.

Social Phobia And Shyness

One difference between social phobia and shyness is the level of anxiety associated with each. There's significantly higher level of anxiety in phobias than with simply being shy. People with social phobias avoid people more severely compared to shy people who can still manage to be with people despite how they feel. Social-phobes, however, can also appear to be outgoing and comfortable in a number of social settings even if they tend to avoid most social settings or feel so anxious about them.

In short, social phobia creates a significantly stronger anxiety compared to simply being shy. Shyness, on the other hand, is comprised of significantly more issues like making new friends, inability to make and maintain eye contact, and having a hard time smiling at other people.

The Hardest Part

When it comes to being shy, what's the hardest part? Truth is, there's no single answer. It really depends on the shy person. For some, it may be making small talk with others. For some, it's making any conversation at all. While for others, the hardest part can be seemingly very easy tasks like making and keeping eye contact while talking to another person or to simply smile and say "hello".

But generally speaking, I think the hardest part about being shy is being unable to enjoy things that you want to enjoy because, well, of shyness.

Sofia Price

Chapter 2 – Are You Shy?

Does public speaking scare the wits out of you? Does the thought of being in front of a crowd become your biggest nightmare? Do you find it difficult to approach people and thus have trouble making new friends? Do you have a hard time speaking your mind?

If you answered "yes" to most of the questions above and to other similar questions, then you are undoubtedly a shy person. Dealing with different social situations is really difficult for you. You often lack the confidence to try something new or to join in activities. Shyness can really hinder you from succeeding in different things or even from simply enjoying life.

The thing is that you are not alone. There are many people who share this same trait with you. Some of them don't mind, but since you are reading this book, you probably do mind. You want to cure yourself of your shyness, or at least want to gain enough confidence to do the things you like.

The Shy Quiz

No, I'm not talking about the quiz being shy. Taking this quiz can help you get a more objective idea if you are really shy or not. Simply answer the questions by rating them according to the following numerical ratings:

-If your answer is never, write 0;

-If your answer is seldom, write 1;

-If your answer is sometimes, write 2;

-If your answer is often, write 3; and

-If your answer is always, write 4.

Here are the questions:

-Are you anxious around people you just met?

-Do you find it hard to come up with things to say to a person you just met?

-Do you find it hard to maintain an ongoing conversation?

-Do you get tongue-tied or stammer during conversations with people you hardly know or have just met?

-How frequently do you feel like you don't have anything much in common with people you interact with?

-Do you find it hard to speak even with people who have the same interests as you do?

-Sometimes, do you get tongue-tied even when you already knew what you were going to say to someone?

-Do you think of sensitive topics after the chance to bring them up has passed already?

-Do you feel left out when you're with your friends or associates?

-Do you think people perceive you as aloof, cold or serious?

-Do you skip parties just because most times, you end up being alone and by yourself?

-Do you feel like a hypocrite when you try to act more social or outgoing?

-Do you find it challenging to talk in front of people or groups of people?

-Do other people remember your name more than you remember theirs?

-Does your speaking voice sound tentative or not confident?

-Do you not laugh or smile as much as you'd want to?

-Do you stand with stiff or tensed pose when with other people?

-Do you find it difficult to make and maintain eye contact with people?

-Do you find it hard to make new friends?

-Do you go out on dates on a lesser frequency than your ideal?

-Do you feel anxious talking to someone of the opposite sex?

-Do you feel anxious conversing with someone from the opposite sex that you find to be attractive?

-Do you find it hard to assert yourself when someone is taking advantage of you?

-Do you find it hard to respond well to someone who cracks a joke that's on you?

-Do you find it hard to ask favor from others?

-Do you find it hard to refuse granting other people's requests from you?

-Do you find it hard to turn down favors asked from you?

-Are you uncomfortable receiving or giving compliments?

-Do you sometimes find it hard to gracefully end conversations?

-Do you think that most people aren't comfortable with silence and that they need to fill the air with meaningless talk just so there's no dead air?

-Do you believe in the saying "the less you say, the less mistakes and the more you say, the more mistakes"?

Tally your total score, which should be no more than 120 points. The range from 0 to 120 represents the degree of your shyness and as such, the higher your score is, the more shy you are. And the more shy you are, the more work you'll need to put into managing or overcoming your shyness, if you decide to do so.

Chapter 3 – Is It Wrong To Be Shy?

I hear some shy people tell others that they like – even love – their being a shy person and that really, there's nothing wrong with being shy. How about you – what do you think? Is it wrong to be shy? Or is being shy just being a normal person? Further, is it best to just accept your being shy and that you are the way you are so that there's no reason nor sense to try and change that? Or would you do something to change it?

Truth is, there's really no need to overcome it. Yes, you read that right – there's really no need to do that...only if you don't want to. It's because being shy isn't a sin, isn't evil nor is it wrong. Being shy also doesn't make you a 2nd or 3rd class earthling. As such, there's no need to be un-shy if you really don't want to. You're free to choose to remain shy or become un-shy!

And because there's no real need to change who you are if you don't want to, many shy people believe there's nothing wrong with being shy. They don't want to do things out of obligation but out of a free heart.

So there you have it – there's nothing wrong with being shy. This however, begs another question: should you just accept being shy? Again, the answer is it depends if you want to or not. However, it isn't that easy for most people.

For one, I believe many shy people who claim to like being that way are actually not satisfied with their confidence levels and social lives. I believe that deep inside, they're not content being isolated, lonely and having just a friend or two around. I believe that most shy people absolutely hate the feeling of being anxious whenever they have to talk to or give a talk in front of other people. And lastly, I believe they hate being unable to make small talk with or ask the person they like out on a date.

I'll go out on a limb here by saying that most shy people really don't like being shy and that they really want to become un-shy but since they can't un-shy themselves, they use the love of being shy as a reason for not being able to overcome their shyness. Take note, I say most and not all.

Saying "I love my being shy." or "I'm a free person so I don't have to do anything that I don't want to...and that includes overcoming my being shy, which I love of course!" becomes a way to justify their continuing to stay shy and inability to overcome it. Saying such things to themselves and others may also be an attempt console themselves for not mustering enough power to be un-shy.

To Be Or Not To Be Shy

Now ask yourself – do you really love being shy or do you want to overcome it and be un-shy? Allow me to do a Keith Barry or The Mentalist thingy – I hear you think aloud that yes, you want to overcome my shyness and be un-shy! Well, it was really easy to get that. Your purchase of this book is obviously a giveaway that you do want to be un-shy!

While it's true that you are under no obligation to overcome your shyness and that being shy isn't equivalent to being the child of the devil, it will be of great benefit to you if you do want to overcome it. And make sure you want to do it not because you want to earn the approval of others. No, do it because you sincerely want to get the most out of your limited time slot here on God's green Earth.

Although being shy is morally neutral, i.e., neither good or bad in and by itself, it isn't beneficial for you either. As I said earlier, it can hamper your efforts and chances of living life to the fullest. As the famous song of the 80s band The Smiths goes, shyness is nice and shyness can stop you from doing all the things in life you'd like to. Believe me, shyness isn't a benefit nor an advantage because it can, as The Smiths sang, hold you back from experiencing life to the fullest.

For one, shy people are normally isolated from most other people and are lonely as a result of such isolation. Many shy people don't have a very good opinion of themselves because of their inability to function normally around people. And consider this poignant point: most people are working at being more social and confident but no one ever worked hard to deliberately be shy and introverted. Why? There's no point nor benefit to the latter. So I'll reiterate again that the only acceptable reason for trying to change from being a shy person to one who's un-shy is because it will benefit you.

Accepting Yourself

Another possible counter-argument to wanting to change into an outgoing and more confident person, a.k.a. un-shy, is the belief that the greatest love of all is loving yourself as you are and not for what you'll be later on. In other words, you need to accept yourself for who you are.

I definitely agree that having a healthy self-esteem is very important and that accepting yourself as you are means no shame or blame on yourself. No shame means:

-You're not ashamed of being not as attractive or popular as your friends or someone else;

-You're not ashamed of being shy;

-You're not ashamed of your looks and instead of frequently checking out how you look in the mirror, you accept your looks for what it is; and

-You're not ashamed you don't have as much of a social life or as many friends as other people and that you don't conceal that fact just to stay accepted.

Remember, being unashamed of who you really are is a big and critical part of being able to overcome the challenges of being a shy person, including feeling inferior to others.

I'd like to point out, however, that there's a great difference between being truly unashamed of who you really are and being hopelessly lazy! Many people either confuse one for the other or use the former to justify being the latter!

I know you're not one of them. Again, the fact that you're holding this book means you want to overcome your shyness. And you are on the right track! In this book, you will find a step-by-step process on how to improve your confidence and eventually overcome shyness.

Chapter 4 – The Cost Of Being Shy

Remember that the only real reason for wanting to change and overcome your being shy is for you to benefit from it and be able to live life to the fullest? Now we'll look at the flip side of being shy, i.e., the cost of being such.

For many people, attending seminars that requires class participation is enough to make them withdraw their registration even if they have to pay the penalty for doing so. Many such people aren't necessarily incompetent or dumb than the people they're gonna attend seminars with. They may even be more accomplished or intelligent than all of them. However, most people are afraid of speaking in front of groups of people and for many shy people, it's like being given the water board treatment in Guantanamo Bay, i.e., it's torture!

How we wish that shyness is just limited to a child trying to hide behind his or her daddy's leg. Unfortunately, it's not. Shyness, up to a certain degree, can affect almost every area of a person's life. Very shy people find it very hard to function normally as our society tends to value the ability to forcefully communicate one's self. Without such ability or those who are apprehensive about communicating forcefully, negative consequences abound.

Most people experience being shy in specific situations, even extroverts. For example, some people are more comfortable with personal conversations with people they just met but aren't with giving talks in public. Some are more comfortable speaking in a large hall full of people but are apprehensive about asking someone they fancy out for a date. The common denominator that determines the situations that make people particularly shy is the issue of control. The less control a person perceives he or she has over a particular situation, the more shy he or she can be. That explains why some people are more comfortable giving speeches – you control your speech and people can't interrupt or question you – instead of one-to-one conversations, where the person you're talking to is free to ask you questions that you may or may not be able to answer correctly.

Occasional shyness hardly impacts a person's life but it is dispositional or chronic shyness that negatively affect a person's life in varying degrees. Truth is, shyness can have an effect on your ability to experience academic, relational, social and career success.

Let's take a look at a person's academic life. A person can't get high grades by simply acing all his or her written exams and academic papers. A great chunk of being able to get high grades is the ability to forcefully and effectively communicate answers and ideas to professors and classmates. One of the biggest challenges for shy people is communicating forcefully. As such, most shy people participate in class discussions and classroom activities, which makes them practically non-existent as far as their professors are concerned. And because they hardly participate in discussions, they don't get high grades on that area. And when it comes to defending their theses or term papers, their inability to communicate forcibly prevents them from getting a high grade or from passing.

Another way it can affect students' grades, especially for younger ones, is reading. Some parents read in their children's report cards such remarks that their children can't read and are very much surprised because at home, their kids are voracious readers. So who is telling the truth? Actually, the reason teachers put that in the report card is because shy children are too shy to read in class and hence, gives the teachers the impression that they aren't capable of doing so. The child gets a grade that's not commensurate to his or her actual skills and abilities only because he or she is too shy to showcase them.

When it comes to college education, shy people tend to go for courses or majors that suit their shy personalities instead of what they're really good at. As such, many shy people aren't able to maximize their God-given talents and settle for a life or career that's much less than what they can have.

Oh, the costs of shyness don't end upon graduation, if it remains unaddressed. In fact, it's where the real costs of being shy can be felt the most. The business world is one that's very competitive – dog-eat-dog if you may call it. As such, there's very little place for shy people at the middle or top. An example would be job interviews. Because most shy people aren't particularly fond of and good at talking to other people, they aren't able to convince most employers to choose them over others for the lucrative but competitive positions. Since they're also averse to competition, they tend to be unnoticed by their superiors and are often passed over for promotions. And even if they are offered a promotion, their shyness often times compels them to turn such promotions down.

Being promoted it means taking on more responsibilities, which often include interacting with even more people. Shy people tend to exercise "shy wisdom" by turning down promotions to avoid increasing contact with more people than their current job. Shy professors at universities or colleges tend to get lower scores on teaching evaluations and may receive less funding for their projects or advocacies simply because their shyness prevents them from being able to forcibly and clearly communicate their ideas and positions.

And you think career is where the cost of shyness ends, you're wrong! It extends to their social lives, including their love lives. A shy person normally don't have the courage to initiate conversations or even carry one that another initiates. As such, they don't have much friends and aren't able ask or convince the person they like to at least go out with them for coffee or whatever. Their being shy keeps them from being able to build good rapport with others and keeps them lonely and isolated.

Indeed, shyness can significantly affect your chances for success in practically all areas of your life – career, academics, social and love life. As such, shy people aren't able to make the most out of the opportunities that come their way and often times settle for something that's way less than what they can be capable of achieving and enjoying.

Chapter 5 – A Story Of Two Boys

Let's start with a story. This is about two boys: Roy and Edward. Note that these characters aren't real, but their story and similar ones happen in real life. Now, the professions of their respective fathers require them to move from place to place every couple of years. This year, they moved to the same town, and the boys will be transferring to the same school, in the same grade, and the same class.

The two boys are equally smart and skillful. However, they differ extremely on one aspect: Roy is quite shy, whereas Edward is the opposite. This became apparent during their break time. Edward immediately made a lot of friends during their first day at their new school – being all smiles, approaching new classmates, and engaging in conversation. On the other hand, Roy stayed seated in his chair, reading a book. He responded to classmates who talked to him with brief answers and didn't seem to make an effort to prolong a conversation.

Roy's shyness doesn't only affect making friends; it also affects his performance in classes. His exam scores are no issue. They are always high, easily making him one of the top students. However, his participation during class discussions is minimal. He never raises his hand, except for questions that no one else knows the answer to. These rare instances only happen during classes that are on the objective side – the questions have a solid right or wrong answer. Moreover, he never joins school activities that involve high levels of human interaction or those that will put him in front of a crowd.

Edward, as you might have predicted, does the opposite. He is enthusiastic about school activities. He loves to join in class discussions, especially on subjects that require voicing opinions. He joins school plays and is a member of the school's marching band. Because of these things, Edward has a lot of friends, even outside their class.

At the end of the year, both Roy and Edward are both among the class' top students. Their exam scores aren't far from each other, but Edward ranks higher than Roy by a few places because of his higher level of class participation.

Were you able to relate to Roy? Situations like these don't end at school. In the workplace and beyond, there will always be times when human interaction is needed. Extreme shyness can hinder success in a number of ways. That's why many people want to overcome it.

So how do you do it? We'll start with that in the next chapter.

Chapter 6 – Getting In Touch With Your Shyness

As we formally start with the process as to how to overcome shyness, there are some things that you should keep in mind. You should realize that curing shyness is neither easy nor simple. You have to be really dedicated to it. You need to give it effort and time, and need to have a strong desire to change. There is no magical cure for shyness that will take it away in a snap. The process doesn't happen overnight. At times, you might find it hard to follow the suggestions, as they would mostly involve pushing yourself out of your comfort zone. This means that you really have to set your mind to making it happen. And if you do, don't give up, no matter what.

Now that that's out of the way, let's start. What is the first step in overcoming shyness? Well, like with many things in life, you won't be able to effectively take steps to address something without first being aware of it. So the first step in overcoming your shyness is to understand your shyness.

To make it easier for you to understand your shyness, let us divide it into multiple steps:

Know The Reasons

The first step is pinpointing the actual origin of your shyness. Different people have different reasons that make them shy. Being shy does not automatically mean that you are an introvert. It also doesn't mean that you don't like yourself. The only definite thing here is that whenever attention is on you, you feel uncomfortable.

So then, what is the source of your shyness? It is quite probable that it signifies a bigger issue. To understand this, you need intrapersonal communication – basically talking to yourself. Don't worry. It's not a crazy thing to do so. Everyone actually does it every day, just silently most of the time – whether consciously or not. You'll have to check yourself. At times, it won't be enough to think – you have to ponder upon yourself to really pinpoint the reason of your shyness.

Here are some things that you can do:

- Use your alone time to think things through. Think back on what made you shy.

- Keep a journal or diary. It's always easier to review or remember things when you write or type them down. Carry around a small notebook and a pen. Or you can do this with your smartphone or any similar device. Whenever a situation arises that makes you shy, take note of it in your journal. If you're asked to do something and you refused because you feel you'd be embarrassed, note it. For each occurrence you noted, try to figure out why you felt shy about it. There might be different reasons. Write these reasons beside or below the corresponding item. At the end of the day, review the things you noted. You're likely to find a pattern. Compare the items in your journal at the end of the week as well. It will give you more things to compare and will better reveal the underlying patterns.

- Discuss it with someone else. Two heads are better than one, and even the most shy of people will have at least one person that they can feel comfortable with – maybe a friend or family member. Talking to another person can give insights that you might not be able to think of by yourself. It gives a different point of view and will make it easier to figure things out. The other person's perception may be right or wrong, but it will surely provide additional data. It's up to you to weigh and compare things to come up with the most accurate conclusion.

There are a lot of reasons that can make a person shy. To help you out, here are some possible reasons:

- You picture yourself as weak. Ever wanted to try something out but didn't because a voice in your head tells you that you won't succeed? You are thinking of yourself negatively. This voice in your head is difficult to block out. However, at the end of it all, that voice is yours, and you can absolutely control what it will say.

- You think too much about how you are perceived – both by yourself and by others. You are so afraid of making mistakes that you grow too conscious of everything you do. Since you are watching yourself closely, you come to the assumption that others are doing so as well.

- Others regard you as shy. You might have been shy as a child, and the people around you put that label on you. You might have actually grown out of it, but those people still categorized you as such. You then tend to accommodate their perception. The thing to remember here is that it is only yourself that you need to accommodate.

The above list is in no way exhaustive, and there are probably more specific reasons, but these are the most common ones. The thing to remember is that whatever the reason you figured out, you can definitely triumph over it. You'll find out how soon enough.

Acceptance

Awareness was the first step. After figuring out exactly what the origin of your shyness is, the next thing to do is to accept it. You might be denying the reason because of certain circumstances. It's time to stop that. You have to get in touch with your personality instead of living in denial. That's because resistance, whether it's conscious or subconscious, won't do you any good. It would be harder to overcome if it's subconscious, but that's taken care of by the awareness part, such that it's now brought to the conscious level. Admit to yourself that you are shy. Only then can you do something about it.

In practical terms, how can you accept your shyness? First, look for the good things in your being shy. One of the ways to do this is by looking back to the past. At the onset, it may not seem that your being shy has led to some remarkable benefits and that you may remember the ways you suffered as a result of it. While that's certainly, well, normal, you have the power to change the way you think about it and actually discover benefits from your being shy.

Next, create a list of those benefits. It seems more natural and easier to jot down the negatives of your being shy but stay the course of listing down benefits of being shy. Some of these can be:

-Being shy allows you to be comfortable to just listen to other people, especially as they pour their hearts out to you;

-Being shy compels you to analyze situations more carefully before getting into something major or important;

-Being shy enables you to listen to other people better and catch what they're really trying to say;

-Being shy gives you the opportunity to get information on your surroundings, like other people's body languages; and

-Being shy helped you develop a richer and deeper inner life and dialogue.

Another way to help you identify the good things associated with your being shy is by journaling. It helps you to document situations or events where your being shy was an asset instead of a liability. Journaling regularly allows gives you the benefit of not forgetting such events as well as being able to go back to them when you want to, particularly on days when you strongly feel bad about being shy.

So what can you journal about? Here are some examples:

-Instances when being shy boosted your career or helped you do your job well;

-Situations where being shy helped you deepen certain friendships or benefited your love life; and

-Moments when you were able to overcome challenges associated with being shy.

Once you're able to identify the good things that came out of your being shy, it's time to start loving yourself. For starters, take deep, long look at yourself in the mirror. What you see is what you get – 100% you. Remember that you are unique – there's no one else on earth exactly like you – and that at some point in your life, you've done some great and wonderful things.

Smile as you look at your reflection in the mirror and be aware of how it feels seeing yourself smile. Don't put yourself down by ridiculing what you see in the mirror or your personality. Simply bask in who you currently are. This is a good way to start loving and accepting yourself – including your shyness. It'll be good to tell yourself the good qualities you possess as you look at your reflection.

Next, why not give yourself a hug! Contrary to popular opinion, you don't need another person to experience being hugged. As long as you have both arms intact, that should be enough for you to experience a hug even when you're alone.

Remember how it feels to have someone hug you – it feels really great, right? If you hug yourself wholeheartedly, you can experience the same feeling! And even better, hugging yourself can help you boost self-esteem and bring down stress levels. You may not be aware of it but doing so can help you enjoy affections associated with being hugged that you haven't experienced in a long while.

It's pretty easy to hug yourself, really. Simply wrap your right arm over your chest and on top of your upper left arm. Then, wrap the left arm over your chest and on top of your upper right arm. Then at the count of 3, give yourself a relatively gentle (or hard, if you prefer) squeeze for as long as you wish. When done, give yourself a pat on your back, which can give you similar benefits as hugging yourself.

Three more ways of truly loving yourself is by sleeping, eating and moving. Doing all three the right way will help you feel and look much better physically. And we all know that physical wellness is greatly linked to how good a person feels about him or herself, which is key to being able to accept your shyness. If you can recall, weren't you in a relatively bad mood when you felt a nagging headache or when you felt really sick with the flu? Now you know why it's important to get and stay healthy.

Eat healthy to be healthy. Truth is, health comprises much of our health and if you eat junk, you'll get a junk body with a junk health that'll make you feel like junk too. Eat more whole foods instead of processed ones. Go for complex carbohydrates instead of simple and processed ones for greater and longer-lasting energy levels. Minimize your intake of fat too.

Get enough exercise to keep your muscles toned and your cardiovascular system in good shape. Regular exercise has been shown to benefit the body in several ways including increased energy, strong muscles and good stamina.

And lastly, get enough sleep, will you? How much is enough? Well, it varies among different people but the consensus is, at least 7 hours nightly is a good average to go for. Some may require less and some more. To get a better feel, try waking up without an alarm clock for the next few days and record how many hours of sleep you got and note how you felt throughout the day. This should give you a good idea of what your optimal sleeping hours are.

Figuring Out Your Triggers

Now that you know and admit that you are shy, the next thing to do is to find out which situations trigger your shyness. When you figured out the reasons for your shyness, you have noted down some situations, but your focus was the root reason. Now, you will again look back at them, but your focus will be on the specific situations.

It's unlikely that you get shy about everything. Most, if not all, shy people are comfortable around their family and/or closest friends. This makes it evident that anyone's shyness isn't a universal thing. Therefore, it is more than possible to overcome.

In listing the situations, you have to be as specific as you can. You will have an easier time pinpointing your triggers if you do so. Consequently, it will be easier for you to conquer your shyness.

Here are some good steps to take:

- As previously mentioned, start with your "shyness journal" – look at the situations that you wrote down. Just list them on a scratch paper for now. You'll see why later. Copy only the situations. You don't need the reasons right now as you have already figured those out.

- Go beyond the journal. Chances are that you didn't start keeping such a journal from when you were a child. So, think back as far as you can remember. List as many situations as you can.

- Once done, review your list. Are there any items that are similar to each other? Are there items that you can further specify (e.g., "talking to people" to "talking to people of high authority" or "talking to people I like")? Refine your list.

- Once you feel your list is refined adequately, rank the items on your list. Base this on how anxious each situation makes you. It's a good idea to quantify them. For example, use a scale of 1–10, where 1 is for the least anxiety caused and 10 is for the most. Arrange the situations from highest to lowest.

Now you know the initial part of the process of overcoming your shyness. Hold on to that list. You'll be using it throughout the whole process. In the next chapter, we will move into conditioning your mindset.

Chapter 7 – Owning Your Mind

Shyness is a manifestation of your mental processes. The mind is very powerful. As you know, the brain controls everything in our body: your voluntary actions (like walking or running) and involuntary actions (including all the necessary functions of your body like circulating blood, breathing, and digestion). As a human, your brain goes through a lot more thinking processes than that of other animals. Humans are conscious beings, and this is why there are shy people.

You might have the physical ability, talent, and/or skills to do something. However, when you think you can't, you won't be able to. This is the major problem confronted by shy people. When they are in a certain situation, their mental processes prevent them from trying things out. This is true even with some things that they like. Thus, shyness can hinder happiness. This is probably why you are reading this book.

Well, since shyness springs forth from your mental processes, it is only logical that the next thing to do is to control these processes. In short, you have to "conquer your mind."

So how do you do that?

Re-Program Your Triggers

The thoughts that arise whenever your "triggers" occur are the ones that make you shy. This is because you think that they are a cause for shyness. This is comparable to what happens in a computer program. When a program receives a certain kind of data, the program responds in a certain way. Well, you can program your mind, too. The difference is that a computer program can be immediately changed – all you have to do is edit the code. Meanwhile, the mind can be a bit more complicated.

Once you decide to change your behavior in response to a particular trigger, it might take a while to complete that change.

Surely, re-programming your mind will be very difficult at the onset. You will feel uncomfortable, but you can't overcome something if you stay in your comfort zone. You have to step out of it. By doing so, you will expand your comfort zone. People have the ability to condition their minds so that their responses to certain things will be changed to the response they want. People who wear contact lenses weren't just able to wear them. They have to overcome a reflex – a natural response wherein the eyelid will close if a foreign object goes near the eye. Otherwise, they won't be able to wear them. It is the same thing with the "sword swallowers" who perform at circuses or entertainment shows. They've overcome the gag reflex. Reflexes are particularly difficult to overcome as they are involuntary (i.e., generally controlled by the body unconsciously) responses of the body, but people are able to do it. How? They do it by believing that they can. It takes time, effort, and constant practice to achieve these things. It's the same with re-programming your response to your shyness triggers.

One way to change your response is by thinking things through. Every time you refuse to do something because you feel shy, pause and think. Is the reason for your refusal valid? How so? Is it really valid, or are you justifying it? The more you think things through, the more you will realize that there really is no reason to be shy.

Couple your thinking with practice. When a shyness trigger occurs, do the opposite of what you have done in the past. For example, instead of avoiding conversations, start them. When a crowd gathers, your shyness might have made you move to a quiet place. Now, instead of that, stay there and talk to people. You might be thinking, "That's easier said than done." That is definitely true. It won't be a walk in the park. It will be uncomfortable for you, likely in extreme levels. But as you keep practicing, you'll find that it gets easier.

Shift Your Attention Away

In the previous chapter, it was mentioned that one reason people become shy is that they are too focused on themselves. Thus, they also think other people are also watching their every move. If this is one of your reasons, you become too worried about how you are perceived. The result is that you keep yourself from doing certain things because you are afraid to be embarrassed.

In order to rid yourself of this habit, you should turn your attention to other people. If your attention is placed elsewhere, you won't be worried about how you come off. Here are some suggestions on how to accomplish this:

- Be compassionate. When you try to understand others, you will stop being concerned about yourself. Compassion, empathy, and sympathy can help you do that. Aside from turning the attention away from yourself, this will help you create harmony with the people around you.

- Another thing you can do is to imagine thinking patterns. Without knowing it, we assume that other people think the way we do. Try to do the opposite. Imagine how people who aren't shy think. You'll realize that they aren't concerned about how they are perceived. Then, you know that they have a different thinking pattern. In time, you will be adopting this thinking pattern without you even knowing.

Visualize Triumph

One thing that makes you shy is thinking that you will fail. So, it will help if you think the other way. Condition yourself into thinking that you will succeed. Visualizing success is one helpful way to achieve this. First, imagine a situation that will make you shy. Now, imagine that you are confident in that situation.

Repeat this visualization often, imagining a different situation every time. For this to be the most effective, do it every day. The recommended time is in the morning before you start your day.

In your visualization, it will help if you involve as many of your senses as possible. Think about how you will sound, how you would feel, etc. This makes it more real.

Maintain Proper Posture

Maintaining good posture is another practice that will help you conquer your mental processes. If you stand tall or sit-up straight, people see you as confident and dependable. As a result, you will also feel that way about yourself. You will also start acting that way.

Scientific studies actually support the mental benefits of good posture. Results show that when people maintain good posture, they feel more confident and/or authoritative. Moreover, there are also physiological benefits: better breathing and stress reduction. As if you need more reasons.

Listen To Yourself

As a shy person, you are reluctant to talk. When you do talk, you probably mumble, or your voice is too low. The person you are talking to would find it hard to understand what you're saying, so you'll have to repeat yourself. This becomes an embarrassing situation, which makes you even more afraid of talking.

Listening to your own voice is good practice that would enable you to avoid this. Sometimes, when you talk to other people, you hear yourself differently. What you thought you have said clearly might not actually be the case.

So, it's good to gain insight into the way you talk. To do this, record your voice while doing mock conversations. It might seem funny to record yourself, but this truly helps. When you play back the recordings, you will hear patterns. You'll see where your voice trails off. There might also be moments when the volume of your voice isn't as loud as you thought. You might hear stuttering. Practice the conversations, trying to correct those moments when your voice isn't clear. Soon, you'll be able to truly speak clearly and with adequate volume.

Avoid Comparing

"Each person is unique." That's a cliché that you will hear a lot. Well, it's a cliché that stands for a reason – it's true. Why is it important for you to understand this? Well, one thing that makes people shy is feeling that they can't measure up to others. That's because they compare themselves to others too much. This might be a part of what makes you shy. Feeling inadequate because of comparisons with others will cause you to be intimidated. Comparing yourself with others is not necessary. As much as possible, avoid comparisons. If ever you find yourself doing this, remember to be objective and realistic. Realize that you are different, and you don't have to measure up to others. Instead, you just have to improve yourself.

Think Of Your Strengths

Focus on your abilities and achievements. Don't wallow on your mistakes and failures. Just take the lessons and move on. This is related to the previous topic. You have abilities, and you can offer something to the world that is different from what others can offer. Think of the things you can do, the things you know, and your past accomplishments. This way, you will know what you can contribute to a group.

As you do this, you'll find that there is a lot you can offer. There are things you can contribute to any situation. You'll realize that there's always something you can do to help. With this in mind, you'll be more confident to express your opinions or simply speak up.

You have your own strengths and value in social situations. The people with the loudest voice and those who appear the most energetic during parties or other social gatherings aren't the only ones that contribute to the experience. You may not be very talkative, but have you ever stopped to think how well you listen? Or maybe you're a good observer. Social interactions need those kinds of people.

Get Rid Of Stereotypes

Clear yourself of stereotypes and labels. Introversion and happiness aren't mutually exclusive things. Extroversion doesn't automatically mean happiness, too. If other people believe in labels, you don't have to accommodate them. There's no point trying to change their opinions either. The important thing is that you know it yourself. Do not let yourself be put inside the proverbial box because of stereotypes. Instead, make it a practice to not use these labels on others as well.

In overcoming your shyness, do things at your own pace. If you push yourself too far, the result might be the opposite of your goal. Do not be forced by what other people say. Allow yourself to be pushed by your own motivations.

Now you've learned some methods as to how to condition your mind towards overcoming shyness. In the next chapter, we move on to more specific steps. You'll learn about dealing with social situations.

Chapter 8 – Social Situations – Being in Control

You'll know that you're succeeding at overcoming shyness when you become more and more comfortable with social situations. In the previous chapters, we've discussed how to understand your shyness and how to control your mental processes. Now, it's time to talk about the things you can do in order to deal with social interactions.

Keep Yourself Well Informed

It's easier to conquer shyness if you can easily join in on conversations. To be able to do that, you must be well informed. The idea behind this is that it will enable you to have the highest chance of having something to contribute. The objective is not to impress others or feign interest in topics that you really aren't interested in, but rather to become friendly.

You don't really need to get out of your way just to be informed. Make it a part of your daily entertainment routine. Watch TV, read articles, or listen to the radio. Do not force yourself to like topics that you're not really fond of, but also try to widen your horizon. If you stay informed, there would be a lower chance for dead air to occur in conversations.

Know The Stages

Social interaction is not an exact science. However, you can simplify it to a certain extent. This will make it easier for you to participate in conversation. Once you grasp the stages of a conversation, you'll eventually be able to do it naturally without thinking about these stages. You can divide any conversation into stages as follows:

1. Opening Stage. As the name suggests, this is where the conversation opens. The so-called "small talk" falls in here.

2. Introduction Stage. You don't need to have this defined, do you?

3. CFOE Stage. CFOE stands for common field of experience. This is where you find the topic/s that the parties in the conversation can talk about extensively.

4. Closing Stage. This is the conclusion of the conversation. One party informs the other that they will be leaving the conversation. If the conversation goes well, it would likely end in an exchange of information indicating the intent to talk again.

Internalize these stages. Analyze the conversations you've been in, and try to pinpoint these parts. Once you familiarize yourself closely with this, you'll be better at handling conversations.

Start Conversations

It will be hard for you at first, but you should do your best to open up conversations with other people. Instead of just waiting for others to talk to you, be the one to approach them. It's probably not as hard as you imagine. Express a random comment about something that you and the person you'll be talking to have in common. It can be anything – the vehicle you're both riding, the food you're eating, the activity you're joining – anything at all. As long as you have good intentions, the other person will feel it and will likely carry on the conversation.

Refine Your Responses

To keep a conversation going, it is important to let the other party feel that you are interested. This will rely heavily upon your responses. If you ask someone a question and he/she gives a one-word response, would you feel that person is interested in talking to you? The same is true for you. Instead of just answering their questions, why not ask a question back? You can also offer up some further comment. You can also do both. It is easier to strike the common field of experience stage this way.

Warm-Up Talk

Try this one out when you attend a party: talk to one or two people at a time. Limit the conversation to two minutes. It's easier to make such short conversations, and it reduces the anxiety you may feel. Repeat until you have talked to everyone. Then, go back to the ones you want to be friends with. This is actually the best use of your time.

Become Totally Approachable

Be approachable. Well, you might be willing to engage in a conversation, but do you appear so? For people to actually think that you're approachable, you must show it through how you act and appear. If you're busy fiddling with your smartphone or another gadget, people won't be likely talk to you, but it's not because they don't like you. They just don't want to disturb you.

You can also show that you would like to talk by keeping a smile on your face. It is easy to do and pleasing to the eye. Smiling at others gives a cue that you are friendly. It is also a really good precursor to opening a conversation. When someone smiles at you, don't hesitate to smile back.

Eye contact is also a big help both in starting and keeping a conversation alive. It takes a good deal of practice to know the right amount of eye contact to make, but you'll eventually figure it out.

You'll also be better at social interactions if you are relaxed. Tension will affect your voice and actions. The person you are conversing with will most likely notice when you are tense. This tension will distract you both from having a good conversation, so it's important to keep your body relaxed.

During a conversation, you may start to feel anxious. When that happens, check yourself. You might not be breathing properly. Breathe slowly, and your body will start to get more relaxed. Check whether your position is comfortable. Shift to a more comfortable one if not.

Now you have insight into how to deal with social interactions. The next stage is to step out of your comfort zone. You won't really go far if you don't give yourself a challenge. That's what we will discuss in the next chapter.

Chapter 9 – The Push

Now, it's time to challenge yourself. Remember, though, that you shouldn't push yourself to the extreme right away. You should take it slowly. Just because you decide to start overcoming your shyness today doesn't mean you should be participating in a public speaking contest tomorrow. Something like that is not realistic, and it will only lead to serious repercussions.

The first thing to do is to set up realistic goals and objectives. Your overall goal is indeed "overcome shyness." But then, this just isn't tangible. In order to accomplish it, you need to support it with specific and tangible objectives. "Initiating a conversation with a stranger" or "talking to my crush" are some good examples of specific objectives.

Start small, and maintain your focus on daily achievements. Don't neglect even the smallest ones, as they will build up and help you eventually overcome your shyness completely.

Do note, however, that while it's recommended to go slowly, you should still set a time limit for yourself. Otherwise, you will just be lax and unlikely push yourself. Thus, you won't get closer to your goal.

Goals And Objectives

Set your objectives according to what will be useful to you. When we say that you should step out of your comfort zone, it doesn't mean that you should be immersing yourself in things that you just can't stand. For example, you don't have to go clubbing or barhopping if that's not really your thing. Even if you are able to immerse yourself in such environments, your practices just won't last long. Perform the recommended steps in settings that would actually be beneficial for your life, such as the workplace or school.

Practice, Practice, Practice

Keep practicing by deliberately placing yourself in social situations that you know will be difficult for you. Apply the things you have learned about conquering social situations. You'll accomplish more and more as time goes by.

One thing you can do is interact with a stranger each day. Give some random person a smile. The longer you do this, the more you will realize that there are a lot of approachable and friendly people out there.

Record Your Success

In this last part, we'll be recommending the journal again. In the initial parts of the process, you used it to record your shyness, its reasons, and its triggers. Now, you will record the instances where you triumphed over them. Like before, review this at the end of the day. This is really beneficial. Having concrete or quantifiable proof of your success adds motivation, and this is what will keep you going.

In your quest to overcome your shyness, you will occasionally go through bumps and roadblocks. Maybe a person will throw off your attempts at conversation. Those times might make you want to give up. That's why you're taking things at your own pace. Pause a little, and remember that learning never ends. Keep going, and you'll eventually reach your goals.

Chapter 10 – Social Anxiety Disorder

You may be wondering, isn't social anxiety disorder and shyness one and the same taco? Although both social anxiety disorder and shyness may have several characteristics in common, they are different. But if you've spent a great chunk of you life being shy, you may not be able to tell the difference between the two. If so, how can you tell which is which? How can you say it's serious enough to be considered as social anxiety disorder.

Also known as social phobia, social anxiety disorder is considered to be an anxiety disorder where a person experiences unreasonable and excessive fear of being in social situations. Extreme nervousness (anxiety) and being self-conscious are the natural fruits of one's fear of being criticized, judged and being watched closely by other people.

Some of the characteristics of suffering from social anxiety disorder include the fear of committing mistakes, being humiliated or embarrassed, and looking bad in front of other people. Lack of experience in social settings as well as inadequate social graces and skills can magnify or worsen this fear, which can turn into a panic attack. Such fears subject people to extreme distress in specific social situations, which either forces them to endure the burden or simply avoid such situations altogether. Incidentally, sufferers of social anxiety disorder tend to experience what is known as anticipated anxiety or the fear of situations that are yet to happen within days or even weeks. For the most part, they are aware of the unreasonableness of their fears but despite such awareness, they're can't overcome them.

People who suffer from social anxiety disorder tend to have false beliefs about other people's negative opinions and social situations. If left untreated, social anxiety disorder can seriously affect a person's ability to go about the day normally, which includes relationships, social activities, work and school.

Most people who suffer from social anxiety disorder fear multiple situations such as:

-Asking questions in a class or seminar or reporting in front of a group of people;

-Being the central focus of people's attention;

-Drinking or eating in the presence of other people;

-Going to public toilets;

-Social interactions, including parties and going out on dates;

-Talking on the phone;

-Working or doing something in the presence of other people;

Social anxiety disorder can be related to various other mental conditions like depression, obsessive-compulsive disorder and panic disorder. Actually, many sufferers from social anxiety disorder often start consulting with doctors not for the manifestation of social anxiety problems but because of other complaints pertaining to it.

And speaking of symptoms...

Symptoms

Initially, people who suffer from this disorder simply feel there's something wrong but aren't able to put a finger on what that is. Typically, social anxiety disorder symptoms include:

-Extreme anxiety during social situations;

-Aversion to social gatherings or situations;

-Physical anxiety symptoms include diarrhea, upset stomach, muscle tension, blushing, shaking, sweating, heart pounding and confusion.

Causes

Social anxiety disorder doesn't have a single identified cause, though scientific researches suggest environmental, psychological and biological factors contribute greatly to the development of this condition in people.

Biologically speaking, social anxiety disorder is believed to be due to a person's brain circuits functioning abnormally, circuits that are responsible for regulating the flight-or-fight response system as well as emotions in general. Because this medical condition has a relatively high chance of occurring in first-degree relatives of people who have it, it is believed that genetics also play a role in its development in people.

Psychologically speaking, it's possible for a person to suffer from social anxiety disorder as a result of extremely humiliating and embarrassing experiences like being ostracized or bullied in school or being scolded regularly in public while growing up.

Even if a person isn't genetically predisposed to the condition or hasn't gone through some extremely humiliating and embarrassing experiences while growing up, he or she can still develop social anxiety disorder when they observe other people's actions as well as the consequences of such like being humiliated or ridiculed publicly, which is a form of borrowed humiliation or ridicule. And it isn't just extremely negative experiences that can lead to development of this disorder. Even the way people were raised by their parents can be responsible for developing such a disorder. For example, sheltered and over-protected children may grow up not learning important social skills due to lack of opportunities to mingle with other children while growing up, which can make them awkward in social situations as adults.

Shy Or Sad?

One reason why many people go through life with undiagnosed – and untreated – social anxiety disorder is because the symptoms are often confused for simply being shy or very shy. As such, they don't seek professional help despite the condition being classified as an official mental disorder with diagnostic criteria.

Although it's true that many symptoms are similar with shyness and social anxiety disorder, the difference lies in the severity or intensity of the symptoms, i.e., severity of impaired functioning, the level of avoidance of social situations and the intensity of anxiety around people. For example, people who suffer from social anxiety disorder aren't merely nervous prior to a speaking engagement. They'll be anxious about it even months prior and as a result, lose sleep over it for until the event has been concluded. During the speaking engagement itself, they may experience intense anxiety symptoms like shaking, profuse sweating, difficulty breathing and intense palpitations. Worse, such symptoms even get worse as the social situation that triggers it progresses. Lastly, people who suffer from it are unable to control such fears despite being aware of the irrationality and baselessness of such anxieties.

Since social anxiety disorder is a an official disorder with diagnostic criteria, screening for it isn't as simple as figuring out if you're a shy person or not. If you suspect you're more than just shy, you need to go to a doctor or some other professional health care provider who will interview you extensively to know if you meet the criteria for a social anxiety disorder diagnosis. The doctor or health care professional may, however, require you to undergo screening to know if you require a more extensive follow-up evaluation.

An example of such a screening is the mini social phobia inventory, or Mini-SPIN for brevity, which is made up of 3 questions only. To complete this, your doctor or health care professional will ask you to rate three statements in terms of their presence in your life from 0, which means "not at all", to 4, which means "extremely present":

-I avoid doing certain things or talking to people out of fear of being embarrassed;

-I stay clear of situations where I'm the center of people's attention; and

-Some of my worst fears include looking stupid or being embarrassed.

If you score a total of more than 5, then it's highly possible that you have social anxiety disorder and the medical health professional may officially diagnose you as indeed having such.

Aside from the Mini-SPIN and it's more extensive sibling, the SPIN, other ways of screening for the disorder include:

-Fear of Negative Evaluation Scale;

-Liebowitz Social Phobia Scale; and

-Social Avoidance and Distress Scale.

Such equipment is indeed a great help in terms of determining possible challenges related to social anxiety disorder but there is still no substitute for a good old complete diagnostic interview done by a doctor or a mental health professional. They can give you their full assessment, or if they can't for one reason or another, they can refer you to others who can.

Sofia Price

Chapter 11 – Social Anxiety Disorder Coping

Social anxiety disorder is clearly not something to be taken lightly or for granted. It is important to know how to cope with well to minimize its effects on your life or the life of your loved ones who may be suffering from it. In this chapter, we'll look at different ways to cope with it.

Baby Steps

There really isn't any other way to proceed with major life changes but through small incremental steps or baby steps. When you look back on how you developed social anxiety disorder, you'll find that it didn't pop up overnight but that it took many small incremental events leading to its full development. As such, shouldn't it be realistic to expect that treating it needs to be incremental too?

When it comes to social anxiety disorder, it may include relaxation exercises that can be mastered only in due time.

Listen To Your Self

Often times, we talk about stuff in our minds that can either be true of false. This is what psychologists refer to as our self-talk. Others, especially the more spiritually inclined and profound people of the world, call it the inner voice. Whether you call it the inner voice or self-talk, this can be positive enough to help boost you boost your self-esteem and manage your social anxiety disorder well. It can also be negative enough to actually trigger or worsen ongoing anxiety attacks and over time can lead to chronic unhappiness. These negative self-talks or inner voices are also called "cognitive distortion" by psychologists. They are called such because these thoughts are considered irrational and distorted.

Unfortunately, almost everyone – you and me included – automatically engage in such cognitive distortions several times during the day and if left unguarded, can result in false assumptions about our behaviors, feelings and thoughts as well as those of others.

The solution is simple: recognize such thoughts as the pop up and rebut or answer them in order to keep such thoughts from putting you down and from triggering your social anxiety.

It's Natural

Strictly speaking, anxiety is nothing but the usual response to anything you think is dangerous. Sensing danger, our mind and body prepare to either fight or run away from the danger by producing the hormone adrenaline, which is a crucial element for optimum performance.

Being concerned about other people's opinions or perceptions is also natural because we as humans are social species, depending on each other for survival. Today, as with the past, social harmony is ensured by our innate fear of being judged or perceived negatively by others in our "tribe".

However, everything natural can also be bad if excessive. These natural feelings can be intensified excessively by both genetics and our environment. Anxiety disorders can be genetic. There are some genes that can make your psychological alarm system become so sensitive as to become disorders. Your childhood experiences, especially those that are extremely humiliating, can also lay the foundation for the development of social anxiety disorder in your life.

It Isn't Real

Social anxiety thrives on thoughts that judge others negatively, that "see" negative outcomes before they even happen and exaggerate danger and these thoughts can significantly affect your energy and mood. Good examples of these would be "I'm gonna blow this opportunity out of the water." and "Here comes the pain!" and these kinds of thoughts can lead to anxiety symptoms such as colds sweat and heart palpitations, among others.

The good news is that thoughts like these are most often than not, habitual. The even better news is you have the power to replace bad habits with good ones. To be able to do this, practice being attuned to what you normally think of and tell yourself whenever you are nervous about a social situation such as entering a room full of people, giving a sales presentation or even as simple as calling a restaurant server to take your order. It's best to document these thoughts as you identify them, possibly via journaling. Also note how anxious you feel during these situations.

It's good to keep in mind that anxious thoughts are often times exaggerations and distortions of seemingly normal concerns like "everybody's staring at me", "I think they smell that I'm not as prepared as I should've been" or "I won't be able to live with the fact that I bombed on this presentation".

The real solution lies in realistic thinking, not mere positivity. As you evaluate your thoughts that produce your anxieties, align them objectively with reality.

Re-Label

In many cases, the symptoms for excitement and anxiety are almost the same. As such, you can re-label your anxious symptoms as excitement. For example, instead of saying "I'm nervous", you can rephrase it into "I'm excited and can't wait!"

Breathe In, Breathe Out

The bad thing about anxiety, one of the many actually, is that you think you can't stop it from building up the moment it starts. Fortunately, deep and slow abdominal breathing can do wonders in terms of easing away anxiety.

To develop this very useful breathing skill, lie on your back and place your hands on top of your abdomen. Through your nose, breathe deeply up to a count of four and as you inhale, allow your abdomen to rise but keep your chest still. Breathe out to a count of 4 at which point your abdomen should already be flat. Keep your breaths to a maximum of 8 per minute.

Once you're used to this exercise, try it sitting down:

-Sit comfortably on a chair, keeping your shoulders relaxed and back straight. Put one hand on your stomach and the other on the chest. This is for you to know how you actually breathe while doing this exercise.

-With your mouth closed, slowly and deeply breathe in through your nose and as you do, gradually count to 10. If you don't make it to 10 at first, don't worry. Simply start with a lower number like 5 and gradually build up to 10.

-As you count while breathing, pay close attention to any sensations your body may feel while breathing in. Your hand that's on top of your chest should remain still and only the hand on the stomach should be moving up and down. If your chest hand moves, it means you're breathing from the chest and not the abdomen.

-After reaching 10 or the lower number you started with, hold in your breath for about a second before slowly exhaling through your mouth. Count to 10 as you exhale all the air you breathed in. Again, if you find 10 to be too long in the beginning, start with a lower number like 5 too. As you exhale slowly, feel yourself pushing all the air out of your mouth, with the stomach hand moving down.

-Repeat the exercise – breathing in through the nose and out through the mouth – and keeping your breathing pattern slow and steady. Do ten consecutive repetitions.

Next, do this standing up and once you've mastered it, practice the technique all throughout the day as you go about your regular schedule. By then, it would've been natural to you already. And whenever you start to feel anxious in social situations, you can consciously switch yourself on to abdominal breathing to ease away the anxiety. As you continue performing this exercise regularly, you'll learn to properly control your breathing to help you ease anxiety symptoms.

Focus Redirection

When you're anxious, you tend to focus inward to yourself. You feel your racing and pounding heart and sense your hands shaking uncontrollably, among other things. These feed your anxiety even further, thus intensifying it.

The best thing to do? Redirect your focus to the activity at hand, be it pouring champagne in a social gathering or giving a toast for the best man during his wedding. If you're conversing with someone, simply pay closer attention to what the other person is telling you and imagine how that person is feeling instead of worrying what to say in response.

If it doesn't work and your anxiety continues to intensify, consider shifting your focus on neutral things like a carpet's texture and color, the feel of your suit's cloth or the rough finish of the room's walls. By shifting your focus, you can break the anxiety build up and be able to relax enough to get back to business.

Embrace Discomfort

Truth is, there will always be things that are very difficult or uncomfortable to do but despite such, will always be worth doing anyway. In particular, you'll need to do things that are very uncomfortable to say the least to help you cope or deal with social anxiety disorder.

When you're ready for doing the hard stuff, you'll be pleasantly surprised to find that you can actually do things you initially thought you can't when anxious. Regardless if the people around you notice your anxiety as you power through doing what you need to do, you'll feel much better.

Embrace Uncertainty

For person with any anxiety disorder, this can be one of the most difficult things to do because uncertainty is one of the biggest reasons for experiencing anxiety. It's a well-known fact that life doesn't always turn out the way we want it to and at some point, you'll come face to face with the cold, hard truth that you only have very limited control over everything that happens in your life.

There's really no pleasant way to go about this. You just gear yourself up and expect the unexpected. The sooner you accept that things can likely turn out different from what you planned, the sooner you'll be able to deal well with social anxiety disorder.

Exposure Therapy

For many people, especially those suffering from social anxiety disorder, the word exposure can be one that's enough to trigger, well, an anxiety attack. For purposes of discussing exposure therapy, it will help a lot to know first what it isn't.

First, it doesn't mean you'll just go out and put yourself in situations that trigger your anxiety attacks without the benefit of preparing well or some techniques to help you manage such exposures very well. Second, it doesn't mean exposing yourself to your greatest anxiety triggers hoping that one day after having been so exposed to them, you'll be acclimatized to them and in the process, overcome them.

Exposure therapy obviously involves such exposures but take note, these are done very gradually (remember, baby steps) and in step with developments in your learning of other coping and relaxation techniques for social anxiety disorder.

Initially, you can do this on a small scale by yourself or with the assistance of a trusted friend or anxiety partner. If for example, one of your social anxiety triggers are socializing at dinner parties, start by going out with a small group of your closest friends first. As you do, carefully take note of how you feel, if you experience anxiety and when they happened, including the things that happened immediately prior to the anxiety episodes and how you were able to neutralize it.

You Can Cope Well

Although social anxiety disorder can be one that seriously affects your quality of life, you don't have to live under its shadow and let it run your life. These days, it's considered a common disorder that is treatable through a combination of self-help coping techniques (such as those outlined in this chapter), medications and psychotherapy, both of which will be discussed in the next chapter.

Chapter 12 – Social Anxiety Disorder Treatment

Since social anxiety disorder is a formal medical condition, it needs to be medically treated. In this chapter, we'll take a look at the different ways this condition can be treated.

Psychotherapy

This type of therapy is considered to be quite effective for treating social anxiety disorder. In particular, cognitive behavioral treatments (CBT) seem to be a very effective, time-limited method. Cognitive behavioral treatments include social skills training, exposure therapy with and without cognitive restructuring, and cognitive restructuring. Most CBTs are conducted within 16 weekly sessions where a person's social anxiety disorder symptoms are either gone or at the very least, significantly reduced.

Often times, the primary ingredient of psychotherapy treatment of social anxiety disorder is exposure therapy, which involves the patient learning about his or her irrational fears (cognitive restructuring), basic relaxation and increasing exposure to the situations that trigger his or her anxiety. Initially, it's done within the confines of the psychotherapist's clinic, doing role-playing. As the patient progresses, he or she is brought out to actual events and environments for gradually increasing exposure therapy.

The good news is psychotherapy's effectiveness in treating this particular anxiety disorder has been scientifically documented by Acrturk et al. in 2009 and by Powers et al. in 2008. As such, you can expect significant relief from its symptoms should you decide to try it out.

Medicine

When it comes to medical treatments for social anxiety disorder, selective serotonin reuptake inhibitors (SSRI) are the primary drugs of choice. These were initially created for treating depression and as such, are often referred to as anti-depressants. Over the years, more and more uses for the drug have been discovered, including treatment of social anxiety. The most common SSRIs are Luvox (fluvoxamine), Prozac (fluoxetine), Zoloft (sertraline) and Paxil (paroxetine). Effexor (venlafaxine), another kind of anti-depressant, can also be used to treat social anxiety.

Normally, it takes about 6 weeks to 8 weeks before their full therapeutic effects are observed in patients. As such, the challenge with these drugs in most cases is dealing with impatience and faithfully following doctors' orders to take the medicines on a daily basis.

There is very little difference in terms of treatment efficacy among these anti-depressants. The choice then becomes the prerogative of the doctor, based on his or her knowledge about the medicines, including their potential side effects. And since relief is generally expected within 8 weeks, talk to your doctor if after taking he meds faithfully for 8 weeks you still haven't experienced relief from your social anxiety.

Other medicines – apart from SSRIs – are also prescribed by doctors to treat social anxiety disorder. These include anti-anxiety medications called benzodiazepines, which are rarely prescribed due its addictive nature and sedative effects. These are prescribed because they can take effect quickly with short-term use, especially during emergency cases like last-second public speeches and engagements.

Another class of medicines used by doctors to help patients relieve social anxiety are called beta-blockers. These work by inhibiting or preventing adrenaline or epinephrine to flow freely, which is the physiological reason for anxiety attacks. Essentially, what beta-blockers do is suppress the physical symptoms of anxiety when it hits, buying the patient some time of relief. Beta-blockers are usually taken as short-term solutions, i.e. temporary fast acting ones, such as the previous example of a last-second speaking engagement. As with benzodiazepines, beta-blockers are generally not recommended for social anxiety treatment and very rarely are prescribed for such.

Chapter 13 – Helping Someone Who Has Social Anxiety Disorder – What Not To Say

Social anxiety disorder is a very serious condition. It can significantly affect a person's life and unfortunately, more and more people are developing the condition.

Social anxiety disorder can result in seemingly endless feelings of uncertainty and fear. What adds to the burden of people who suffer from such are the insensitive comments of many well-meaning people surrounding them. Despite the intention of helping social anxiety disorder sufferers experience relief and rest, trying to say what they think is helpful can actually backfire and even make the anxiety attack worse. Social anxiety disorder can be likened at times to quicksand in the sense that the more people try help in relieving the symptoms with what they feel are encouraging statements, the worse it can become. For example, telling a panicking person to be calm is like pouring gasoline on a bonfire.

If you have loved ones who suffer much from social anxiety disorder, you may want to do everything that you can to help them experience significant relief from their misery. And one of the ways you believe can help is by talking them into calming down. While that is commendable, bear in mind that you have to be very careful with what you say so you don't make matters worse.

Here are some of the worst things you can say to someone suffering from social anxiety disorder.

"Don't Sweat The Small Stuff"

There are some things in this world whose benchmarks are very subjective. Take for example the word "small". To people as tall as the NBA's Roy Hibbert and Tim Duncan, both of whom stand close to 7 feet tall, a 6-foot guy is small. To a person who stands as tall as the NBA's Nate Robinson or Mugsy Bogues, the same 6-foot guy is a giant.

When it comes to what is considered small stuff, it may also depend on the person looking at the situation if it really is small stuff or big stuff. For a person suffering from social anxiety disorder, merely entering a room full of people he or she doesn't know is already big stuff – big enough to at least trigger social anxiety symptoms. For those of us who don't suffer from the same disorder, that is really small stuff.

As such, never ever comment to a person who suffers from social anxiety disorder that he or she shouldn't be sweating the small stuff. Even if your intention was noble, it can actually make the person more anxious and instead of helping him or her, you worsen their plight.

Remember what your folks used to say about putting yourself in another person's shoes? Well, I'd recommend the same for your loved ones who suffer from this condition. Try and get into their belief system and try to see the world the way they do, which can help you word your encouragement better so you don't make them more anxious.

"Calm Down"

Have you ever considered the logic behind putting out a fire using gasoline? Hmmm...me neither. It's the same logic behind telling people suffering from social anxiety disorder symptoms to "calm down". Remember, this is a medical condition that has a physiological component to hit and the reason it's called a disorder, among other things, is that the person suffering from it has no real control over the symptoms. So telling them to calm down in the middle of a social anxiety disorder episode will only make them feel even more anxious, like gasoline to a flame!

Most well-meaning people aren't able to think much when one of their loved ones suffer from social anxiety attacks – at least enough to see the obvious that if their loved ones can actually stop their social anxiety symptoms at will, they wouldn't be experiencing them at that moment. It may even seem to some that the person actually chooses to go through the symptoms!

A better alternative to help calm them down? According to esteemed Stanford University professor Keith Humphreys, you're better off asking the person who's experiencing social anxiety symptoms what they'd want you to do together with them that can help ease their anxiety attack. Things like going for a run, brisk walk or a bike ride can help.

"Just Do It"

There are situations that require tough love and then there are some that get worse with it. Experiencing a social anxiety attack is one of them. Again, if people suffering from social anxiety disorder actually have the power to stop it, don't you think it would've been over by now? Better yet, would it have even happened at all? They'd just will the social anxiety symptom into submission for instant relief. Remember, no person in the right state of mind will deliberately choose to experience social anxiety symptoms just for kicks or for the enjoyment of it. Believe me, such symptoms are anything buy joyful or cool.

A much better alternative to telling such people to "just do it" or to "suck it up" is empathy. Telling such people – during a social anxiety attack – that it's a bad feeling to have or that you're sorry they have to go through that may help them feel someone can relate or understand what they're going through and can go a long way towards helping relieve the symptoms.

"Everything's Gonna Be Just Fine"

Despite the noble intention of giving emotional support to someone suffering from social anxiety attacks, it really won't make much of a difference for the person. Why? No one really believes that – that's got to be the most overly optimistic and Pollyanna-ish statement in the history of mankind! Sure, given that it may help the person relax for several seconds but it can just be a matter of seconds before their anxiety attacks again.

A better suggestion would be to continue encouraging the person but not with the use of general statements that are vague and obviously not true. It may even be better to just encourage them to accept and embrace their anxiety and that it's alright to feel the way they do because it isn't their fault.

"I'm Stressed Out Too"

Just like telling an already anxious person to not "sweat the small stuff" and to "calm down", telling them that you're just as stressed out as they are can also worsen the situation instead of helping to neutralize it. Why? It's because by saying that, you inadvertently send the message to the other person that he or she is overreacting because despite being just as stressed out, you're not experiencing a social anxiety attack. It's like telling that person that he or she is such a wuss!

"Let's Go Get A Drink"

Alcohol may help reduce the anxiety in the short term, but when addressing social anxiety disorder, what is needed is a holistic and long-term solution, which includes doctor-prescribed medicines and treatments. Alcohol may develop addiction in the person and can make things much worse over the long term. So next time you feel like you're doing your friend a favor by quenching the anxiety with a bottle of really cold beer, do that friend a favor by ditching the idea and instead, support him by referring him to a medical health professional, if he hasn't seen one yet.

"Was It My Mistake?"

It's very hard to witness a loved one continually suffering from social anxiety disorders and at times, it may seem that you're the one causing his or her social anxiety symptoms. You must consider the fact that anxiety disorders are triggered or caused by things that are much bigger than a single minor event.

It's best for you, as a loved one, to just acknowledge that you have no control whatsoever over what your loved one with social anxiety disorder may feel. Disregarding this advice and trying to control your loved one's emotions will only lead to frustration on your end and your loved one to feel rejected – both of which can lead to resentment and a strained relationship. Just remember not to take their condition personally.

More importantly, you should inform that loved one you are there to support them as they go through doctor-prescribed treatments and therapies to help them deal with their social anxiety disorder well.

Chapter 14 – Success Story

Make no mistake about it – overcoming shyness and social anxiety disorders are not easy feats. It may only seem like it is for those who haven't really experienced it but for those who have gone through them and are still going through them, it's a very daunting and difficult challenge to overcome. It is however, one that can be overcome. Take the story of one of the most successful and richest people in the world, who used to struggle with social anxiety disorder, particularly when speaking in public and giving presentations. His name? Warren Buffet.

With the amount of success he has attained as potentially the most successful fund manager in the history of the world, the Oracle of Omaha certainly has what it takes to make very powerful presentations to many of the world's richest people and institutions. If he isn't anywhere near good at public speaking and giving presentations, there's practically no chance of him being able to convince clients to trust him with billions and billions of dollars of their money.

But here's the funny thing about Warren Buffet – he used to fear public speaking and giving presentations so much that at some point, he would literally get sick prior to speaking or presenting in public, he admitted in one interview. While he was in high school and college, he would choose courses that don't require speaking in public and giving presentations in class. He also admitted to once dropping out of a public speaking class even before the first day came around.

He, however, decided not to let the anxiety conquer him but that he will conquer that anxiety. He eventually enrolled in – and finished – a 1-week public speaking class and soon after that, took on a teaching job at the University of Omaha because he was wise enough to know that only by continuing to expose himself to those trigger situations (exposure therapy) can he maintain his victory over his social anxiety disorder of speaking in public and giving presentations.

Warren Buffet advises people who are suffering from anxiety to force themselves to get into situations that will force them to develop the abilities to successfully manage their anxieties. Take it from him, the Oracle of Omaha who won over social anxiety disorder that helped him become the billionaire he now is.

With Warren Buffet's success story, be encouraged that even though shyness and social anxiety disorder can be one tough challenge, it can be overcome with enough determination, the right treatment and the support of loved ones. It may keep you from living life normally at the beginning but as you continue hacking away at it, you'll find that it isn't just possible to live a normal life – you can also live a very successful one.

Conclusion

Thank you again for purchasing this book! I sincerely hope that you received value from it.

I hope this book was able to help you to gain valuable insight toward overcoming shyness. The next step is to put yourself out there and apply what you have learned in this book.

Finally, if you enjoyed this book, then I'd like to ask you for a favor, would you be kind enough to leave a review for this book on Amazon? I want to reach as many people as I can with this book and more reviews will help me accomplish that!

Thank you, and good luck!

Sofia Price

70620166R00049